Strange Buildings

Dawn McMillan

This house is a building.

This school is a building.

Do they look strange?

NO!

Have you seen a strange building?

THE WOODEN SKYSCRAPER

WHERE: RUSSIA

This is a strange building.
It is the tallest wooden house
in the world!

THE NARROW HOUSE

WHERE: THE NETHERLANDS

This is a strange building.
It is also a house.

Would you live in a very thin house like this?

THE FALLING DOWN BUILDING

WHERE: USA

This is a strange building.
It is a museum.
It looks like it is falling down!

THE CROOKED BUILDING

WHERE: POLAND

This is a strange building.
It is part of a shopping centre.

THE UFO HOUSE

WHERE: TAIWAN

This is a strange building.
It was part of a holiday camp.

THE BUBBLE HOUSE

WHERE: FRANCE

This is a strange building.
It is a house.
The rooms are round.

THE BOOKCASE

WHERE: USA

This is a strange building.
It is part of a library.

THE BASKET BUILDING

WHERE: USA

This is a strange building.
People work here.
They sell baskets.
The building looks like a basket!

THE UPSIDE DOWN BUILDING

WHERE: USA

This is a strange building.
It is a museum.
There are even rides
in the building!

THE POLE HOUSE

WHERE: AUSTRALIA

This is a strange building.
It is a house.
It is built on a pole.
The house moves in the wind!

Would you live in this house?

THE ICE HOTEL

WHERE: SWEDEN

This is a strange building.
It is built from ice and snow.
The beds are made of ice blocks!

Would you sleep in this building?